CROSVILLE
A NATIONAL BUS COMPANY

Michael Hitchen

First published 2019

Amberley Publishing
The Hill, Stroud
Gloucestershire, GL5 4EP

www.amberley-books.com

Copyright © Michael Hitchen, 2019

The right of Michael Hitchen to be identified as the Author of this work has been asserted in accordance with the Copyright, Designs and Patents Act 1988.

ISBN 978 1 4456 9271 5 (print)
ISBN 978 1 4456 9272 2 (ebook)

All rights reserved. No part of this book may be reprinted or reproduced or utilised in any form or by any electronic, mechanical or other means, now known or hereafter invented, including photocopying and recording, or in any information storage or retrieval system, without the permission in writing from the Publishers.

British Library Cataloguing in Publication Data.
A catalogue record for this book is available from the British Library.

Typesetting by Aura Technology and Software Services, India. Printed in the UK.

Introduction

Crosville or 'Crosville Motor Services Ltd', to give its full title, will be a familiar name to many enthusiasts, or individuals over a certain age across large parts of the North West and north and mid-Wales. For those not so familiar, Crosville was a state-owned giant; only London Country and Midland Red owned more vehicles, and only Western National/Devon General operated across a larger area. From its head office at Crane Wharf in Chester, it operated garages as far apart as Holyhead, Macclesfield, Oswestry and Newcastle Emyln in far south-west Wales, at its peak owning thirty-two garages. Once the operating area had been enlarged by the transfer of parts of the North Western Road Car Company and some West Wales services from Western Welsh and South Wales Transport under the 1972 National Bus Company reorganisations, the fleet contained over 1,200 vehicles.

Unique among the NBC constituents, Crosville was named after its founders, Chairman George **Cros**land-Taylor and Georges **Ville**, a French car maker. The early history of the company has been covered by the two books *The Sowing and the Harvest* and *State Owned without Tears*, both by Mr W. J. Crosland-Taylor. Originating in 1906 as a car building company, it grew rapidly as a PSV operator. Then, in 1929, the company was taken over by the London, Midland & Scottish Railway. In 1930, the LMS sold 50 per cent of its shares to the BET Group. In 1942, the company became Tilling-controlled and the livery was changed from red to the well-known Tilling Green. Interestingly, Chester Corporation Transport had been green and upon the Crosville livery change reacted by changing its buses to red! Following the 1947 Transport Act, the British Transport Commission took over the Tilling Group and this process toward full nationalisation of the country bus operators was completed with the formation of the National Bus Company on 1 January 1969. In 1972, the NBC introduced its corporate livery, and this period onwards until the deregulation of 1986 is covered by this book.

The Crosville fleet in the 1970s and 1980s was documented in the company's own fleet list, issued in 1971, 1972/3, 1974, 1976 and 1982. After 1982, PSV circle and A. M. Witton's *Fleetbooks* (which ran to five editions) filled in the gaps. Like other former BET/Tilling companies, Crosville's fleet was mainly made up of Bristol/ECW products, with larger numbers of Bristol MWs, Lodekkas and REs. The National Bus Company brought in many new standard types such as Leyland Nationals, Grant Leyland Leopards, and also the unusual purchase of 102 Seddon Pennine buses and local coaches. Apart from one example at Midland Red, Crosville was the only other NBC user of these vehicles. The biggest change to the fleet was the 1972 boundary change that brought the Cheshire operations of the North Western Road Car Co. into the company, with three garages and over 200 vehicles. At the same time Western Welsh operations in West Wales came into the Crosville fold as well, bringing a variety of non-standard (to the company) types into the fleet. This period is one of the most interesting, in terms of fleet make-up, in the company's recent history.

In the mid-1970s vehicle types were much localised; even the short distance between Crewe and Northwich garages would appear like two different fleets. Similarly, the company's English and Welsh operations also had distinct differences. Bristol SCs and MWs soldiered on in Wales long after they disappeared from Cheshire's roads; the rear-entrance Lodekka remained common in Chester, Wrexham and North Wales when unknown at other garages; and the introduction of the Bristol VRT took a long time to reach Crewe Garage. Even in the 1980s, the fleet maintained much interest with the downgrading of white coaches to dual purpose; the purchase of second-hand dual-purpose types and high-bridge double-deck buses from Southdown and South Yorkshire PTE. It was this rich fleet that made the company so interesting. The Central Workshops in Sealand Road, Chester, a short distance from the Crane Wharf head office, was a fascinating location, with withdrawn vehicles, new types and other NBC vehicles being used for spares, along with a mixture of service vehicles. Such locations have been lost to history.

I have illustrated the fleet as it was in the corporate era, 1972–86, arranged in the order of company's own official publications, i.e. single-deck, double-deck, then service vehicles. Where numbers were reused I have grouped them together, with the odd exception, such as a couple of ex-NWRCC Alexander-bodied AEC Reliances, and a few types delivered close to 1986. The majority of vehicles types used are illustrated, hopefully giving the reader an understanding of the fleet throughout this era.

It is sobering to reflect that this once proud name, with its eighty-year history, has been lost in its true form for thirty-three years. Though the company posted information warning of the forthcoming deregulation plans, I clearly remember with horror the first time I saw a dark green and orange ENL Leyland National, and with it the realisation that the familiar sight of NBC leaf green was not going to last indefinitely! The company did change to a more pleasing green/cream colour scheme, but the fleet soon became tatty, with constant livery variations, vehicle changes and transfers. The Government's ill-conceived deregulation would then see the company initially split in two, then fragmented by a number of sell-offs, often driven by property values, soon after seeing the name disappear altogether – contrary to the Government's own campaign capitalising on selling off NBC Famous Names! Eventually, 'Crosville' would only be found on a couple of former company social clubs. It would be interesting to ponder on what advances would have been made in the last three decades with a state-owned, integrated transport system in what may have been a more progressive Britain.

I must thank Pete Thorley for assistance in completing this book, not only for help with photographs, but for his extensive knowledge on the company's operations. Thanks also go to Merfyn Jones for his Service Vehicle photos and to Richard Morant and the Transport Library (www.thetransportlibrary.co.uk)

I hope the reader will get some enjoyment looking back to a simpler time when the Leaf Green Crosville bus could be seen across diverse landscapes from Snowdonia and the holiday resorts of North Wales to Merseyside conurbations, through the Cheshire Plain and high peaks, the industrial landscape of Wrexham and beyond into the rural Welsh hinterland.

ERG 1 (OFM 1E), Wrexham Bus Station

ERG 1 was allocated to Corwen Garage and had the honour of carrying number one in the single-decker fleet. A batch of six (ERG 1–6) Bristol RESL6G/ECW DP42Fs new in 1967, they spent much of their lives allocated to Welsh garages.

ERG 2 (OFM 2E), Dolgellau Garage

Another member of this batch is seen at Dolgellau Garage, which consisted of a small building; most of the allocation would stand in the yard. In 1967 the company also took delivery of three similar bodied RESL, but finished as buses (SRG 23–25).

SNL 15 (NTU 14Y), Runcorn Garage, 2 Oct. 1983

SNL 15 is carrying the orange T livery, applied to Runcorn vehicles to promote the Busway, which operated service numbers prefixed with the letter T. Crosville only purchased fifteen Mk 2 Leyland Nationals; all were with dual doors. SNL 1–5 came in 1981 and the second batch, SNL 6–15, in 1982/3, included SNG 10, the single example experimentally fitted with a Gardner engine instead of the Leyland version.

SRG 22 (SFM 22F), Crewe Town Centre, 1978

SRG 22 was a Bristol RELL6G fitted with an ECW B53F body, in a batch of thirteen new in 1967 (SRG 9–22); it has the flat front and deep windscreen styling of the period. It was transferred to Biddulph from Crewe in 1975 and is seen about to turn into Crewe Bus Station with the Saturday only K72 from Congleton, which only made two round trips on the day.

ELL 24 (DDM 24X), Chester Bus Station, 9 Sep. 1981

Part of a batch of fifteen (ELL 20 – 34), new in 1981/2, ELL 24 was a Leyland Leopard fitted with Willowbrook C47F bodywork. This batch was delivered new as dual-purpose vehicles, initially in corporate half leaf green/white and registered with a 1980 'W' plate, but they were returned to Willowbrook for rectification work, upon return they were re-registered and received a revised two-tone green DP livery.

CRG 26 (OFM 26E), Biddulph Garage, Sep. 1974

The shared ownership of Biddulph Garage is apparent in this September 1974 view of CRG 26, SRL 236 (KJA 302G) and PMT 108 (PVT 108F). Crosville was a large user of the Bristol RE with coach body, with both single coach and folding double doors, though all had the same style route destination box. CRG 26 was in the 1967 delivered batch of four, numbered CRG 26 – 29.

CMG 35 (OFM 35E), Chester Zoo, 1974

Crosville had two batches of Bristol MWs (CMG 30 – 36, CMG 557 – 570) with this restyled coach bodywork in 1966/67. They were unique to Crosville, which specified the bodywork to fit with a Lodekka-style engine grill. In 1973, Crosville had painted these vehicles in corporate NBC dual-purpose livery, but repainted them into Central Activities white livery soon afterward, which they retained until disposal.

CMG 35 (OFM 35E), Chester Sealand Road Workshops, 1980

The same vehicle is seen again, this time at Sealand Road central workshops in 1977. CMG 35 was the penultimate Bristol MW vehicle from a total of 236 that the company had bought from the late 1950s onwards.

CTL 37 (A37 SMA), Cardiff Bus Station, 8 May 1986

Seen at Cardiff Bus Station after working the long-distance 'TrawsCambria' 701 service from Rhyl, via Aberystwyth and Swansea. CTL 37 was a Leyland Leopard fitted with the impressive Duple Laser bodywork. Delivered in 1983, it was finished in the 'Town Lynx' dual-purpose livery of the period, though some other NBC operators painted them as white coaches.

ERG 40 (UFM 40F), Northwich Bus Station, 1980

In the late 1970s, Crosville started to downgrade National white coaches to dual-purpose status, long after other NBC companies had started this process. Northwich Garage's ERG 40 looks superb as it turns in the bus station, prior to an excursion.

SRG 50 (UFM 50F), Anglesey

Crosville's 1968 delivery of long Bristol REs, was formed of three body types, all from ECW: SRG 42–51 (B53F), ERG 52–61 (DP50F) and SRG 62–71 (D48D). Anglesey allocated single-door variant, SRG 50 to collect passengers while crossing the island on the N1 Amlwch–Holyhead service. (Pete Thorley)

ERG 61 (UFM 61F), South Cheshire, Summer 1981

Crewe's ERG 61 works to Bridgemere Wildlife Park. Close to the Staffordshire and Shropshire border. The K69 was introduced with the MAP changes of November 1980, an infrequent service from Crewe via Shavington and Wybunbury, running Saturdays only, twice a day as far as the Wildlife Park (only in summer 1981). A third service terminated short at Blakenhall Farm, which was also the limit of the winter service. From 1982, it would run only to Blakenhall Council Houses. (Pete Thorley)

SRG 75 (XFM 75G), Brookhouse Estate, Crewe

1968 also saw the delivery of thirty short Bristol RESH6GS with ECW B46F bodies (SRG 72 – 101). Crewe's SRG 75 stands at the southern end of the cross-town K1 service, which ran between two housing estates: Brookhouse Estate, seen here, and Leighton Park in the north. (Pete Thorley)

SRG 90 (XFM 90G), Saron, near Denbigh

In scenery typical of Crosville's rural Welsh operations, Denbigh Garage's SRG 90 climbs towards Saron on the M61 to Waen Nantglyn from Denbigh. (Pete Thorley)

SRG 101 (XFM 101G), Llangollen
Corwen Garage's SRG 101 waits in Llangollen to work the irregular D95 service, which only ran all the way to Corwen twice on Tuesdays, Wednesdays and Fridays. (Pete Thorley)

ERG 104 (AFM 104G), Chester, Sealand Road Workshops, 1980
The company's 1969 Bristol RELH deliveries with coach bodies totalled ten (CRG 102 – 111). All had received NBC white liveries once the 1972 corporate livery had been introduced. A number were later downgraded to dual-purpose vehicles from 1978, receiving corporate green/white as seen here. ERG 104 is also carrying the 'TrawsCambria' board, for use on the long-distance Welsh services. ERG 104's final allocations were Rhyl and Aberaeron and withdrawal would come in December 1980.

SRG 113 (OFM 113E), Corwen Garage, 1983

Locally allocated Bristol REs SRG 113 and dual-purpose ERG 276 are seen at Corwen Garage in 1983, along with Wrexham's SNL 562. The 1969 delivery of Bristol RE buses contained SRG 112 – 127 with ECW B53F bodywork and SRG 128 – 143 with the dual-door forty-eight-seater bodywork.

SRG 135, Runcorn Busway, *c.* **1980**

SRG 135 was a Bristol RELL/ECW B48D of 1969. Carrying the orange 'T' livery specially applied for the services over the Runcorn Busway Network, such as service T9 Shopping City. Runcorn was one of the last Crosville garages to operate Bristol RE buses.

SLP 148 (CFM 148G), Llanidloes, Mid-1970s

SMG 447 and ERG 276 stand over between duties with Bristol LH/ECW B45F SLP 148 at Newtown. SLP 148 and Bristol MW SMG 447 are both from Oswestry Garage, and were on the D75 Newtown/Shrewsbury services, while Corwen Garage's dual-purpose Bristol RE ERG 276 works the 871 Liverpool to Cardiff.

ERG 160 (EFM 160H), Aberystwyth, 1982

1970 was the last year Crosville took delivery of the Bristol REs with the classic 36-foot coach bodywork in this style. A batch of five, CRG 160–164 (EFM 160–164H), were all downgraded to ERG dual-purpose status in 1979/80. ERG 160 displays its 'DeCambria' local fleetname. (Pete Thorley)

ERG 162 (EFM 162H), Oswestry Bus Station

With the Oswestry Garage in the background, Oswestry's ERG 162 departs from the bus station, which was located alongside the former Cambrian Railways station, for its long journey to Manchester. Oswestry was Crosville's only garage in Shropshire, a county served by Midland Red and numerous independents. (Pete Thorley)

SRG 167 (EFM 167H), Chester Bus Station, June 1977

1970 saw Crosville take delivery of a large batch of Bristol RELL (SRG 165 – 224) with both single- and double-door versions; the body front was restyled as well with the flat front being replaced by a curved version. SRG 167 of Rock Ferry Garage displays the MPTE logo after the fleetname, in common with other Merseyside-allocated vehicles.

SRG 174 (EFM 174H), Aberaeron Garage, *c.* **1982**
Another from the flat-front, single=door batch, SRG 174 has the 'DeCambria' local identity introduced as a result of the MAP scheme, and applied to vehicles at Aberystwyth, Aberaeron and Newcastle Emlyn garages.

SRG 177 (EFM 177H), Liverpool City Centre, *c.* **1980**
The first Bristol RELL with the restyled front, SRG 177 heads to Chester via Runcorn on the H21 service. SRG 177 would finish its time with the company in more rural surroundings, allocated to Blaenau Ffestiniog Garage.

SRG 188 (HFM 188J), Crewe Town Centre, *c.* 1983

Once a common sight around the town, Crewe had a number of these B48D versions for its cross-town services. Here SRG 188 works the K12 to the railway station. SRG 185 – 204 were finished with the dual-door body.

SRG 191 (HFM 191J), Blakenhall Farm Turning

Previously numbered K82, the Blakenhall Farm service only operated on Fridays, with two return services from Crewe Bus Station. Crewe's SRG 191 pulls out of the reversing point before the blind was changed to 'Crewe Bus Station'. Crosville in the 1970s had numerous services that operated just a few times a week, often on market days, serving remote rural locations, offering an invaluable service to many communities. (Pete Thorley)

SRG 191 (HFM 191J), Crewe Town Centre, c. 1983

SRG 191 is seen again just after leaving the bus station, again for the railway station. The back wall of the garage can be seen in the background. Purpose built in 1960, in an ideal arrangement, the garage and bus station were located together, though sadly this is not the situation today, with privatisation dispersing facilities.

SRG 194 (HFM 194J), Crewe Town Centre, c. 1983

In 1976, Crewe had an allocation of seventeen SRGs, of which ten were the dual-door version. Two of these – SRG 194 in front of the garage whilst SRG 188 works the K2 for Leighton Hospital – are seen here in front of the bus station bays in the early 1980s.

SRG 194 (HFM 194J), Crewe Garage, *c.* 1973

SRG 194 is seen again, on the K1 railway station service, carrying the 'farebox' slip-board, a self-service system where passengers dropped their fare into a cast farebox. It relied on passengers having the correct change for a quick service.

SRG 199 (HFM 199J), Runcorn Depot

With its urban dedicated busway system, it is no surprise that Crosville's largest allocation of SRGs was at Runcorn, with thirty in 1976, and twenty-three by 1982. A long-term resident of Runcorn, SRG 199 was seen in the Busway orange 'T' livery.

SRG 203 (HFM 203J), Crewe Town Centre, c. 1983

Back in Crewe, SRG 203 stands on one of the bus station's through-platforms. These were used by the cross-town services, which would call briefly, making use of the bay platforms impractical. K1 ran between Leighton Hospital and the railway station.

SRG 206 (HFM 206J), Pwllheli Bus Station, Mid-1970s

Working the R12 Caernarvon to Pwllheli, SRG 206 stands at Pwllheli Bus Station. Crosville occasionally painted its vehicles in all-over advertising as an additional source of revenue and SRG 206 is carrying a striking advert for Jeff's Plumbing Supplies of Colwyn Bay. This vehicle had also been painted in all-over advertising for Red Garages in 1973. It would be painted in standard NBC green in the 1980s.

SRG 226 (KJA 303G), Wrexham Garage, 1979

The takeover of North Western Road Car Co. in 1972 brought a number of non-standard vehicles into the fleet. The chassis was familiar to Crosville, the Bristol RESL, but the Marshall body was not. These vehicles (SRG225 –232) had initially stayed at their original garages, SRG 226 at Macclesfield, but later some could be found on unfamiliar territory, such as here at Wrexham Garage.

SRG 232 (KJA 309G), Biddulph Garage, Oct. 1974

Eight former North Western Marshall-bodied Bristol RESLs came to Crosville, SRG 225 – 232, fitted with Marshall B43F bodies, noticeably shorter than the similar ex-NWRCC Marshall-bodied SRL batch. Biddulph Garage's sole example, SRG 232, stands alongside the garage in 1976.

SRL 235 (SJA 360K) and SRG 230 (KJA 307G), Macclesfield Garage, Nov. 1974

The entire ex-NWRCC Bristol RELL/Marshall B49F batch that came to Crosville in 1972, SRL 233–237, were allocated to Macclesfield Garage. SRL 235 stands inside the garage, in company with SRG 230; though similar from the front, they differed in body length.

SRL 237, Macclesfield Garage, Oct. 1976

The longer body of this batch is illustrated in this view of SRL 237 in Macclesfield Garage, in company with a Daimler Fleetline DDG, also ex-NWRCC, and a new Leyland National dual-purpose ENL.

SRL 242 (SJA 387J), Warrington Arpley Bus Station

Twenty-one Bristol RELLs with more familiar ECW bodywork also came with the NWRRC takeover. Nine were fitted uniquely, with low-height bodies (SRL238 – 246) specially built to allow them to fit under a canal aqueduct near Dunham Massey. SRL 242 stands in Warrington Arpley Bus Station, alongside the closed LNWR railway station.

SRL 252 (SJA 379J)

The remaining twelve ex-NWRCC Bristol RELLs, SRL 247 – 258, had standard ECW bodywork. Apart from the L indicating a Leyland engine in the SRL vehicle code, this Bristol RELL initially appears the same as Crosville's own 1970 intake, but they were recognisable by their red seats and the small lower window in the rear emergency door. SRL 252 travels through mid-Cheshire, en route for its home garage. (Pete Thorley)

SRL 258 (SJA 393K), Congleton Aqueduct

The standard ECW body SRLs were divided between Northwich (seven) and Macclesfield (five) garages for much of their time. SRL 258 passes under the Macclesfield Canal at Congleton Aqueduct; the K91 was a Congleton Town circular service. Congleton gained an outstation after the sudden closure of Biddulph Garage by PMT. (Pete Thorley)

ERL 264 (TFM 264K)

ECW restyled its coach body in 1971. Crosville took its first delivery of ten in 1972, numbered CRL 259–268; they had an austere appearance. All were painted in National white. By 1982, eight had been downgraded to dual-purpose and re-classed, such as ERL 264, seen while on National Express working 804 to Birmingham.

CRL 268 (TFM 268K), Cheltenham Coach Station, 1973

Still in National white, the last of the 1972 batch, CRL 268, turns into Cheltenham Coach Station while working service 647, part of the Associated Motorways network, which Cheltenham served as a hub for connections.

ERG 269 (YFM 269L), Rhyl Bus Station, Oct. 1983

Delivered in 1972/3, a batch of twenty-four bus-bodied Bristol RELLS were fitted with dual-purpose seats. Numbered ERG 269–288 and ERL 289 – 292, the last four were fitted with Leyland engines.

ERG 281 (YFM 281L), Sealand Road Workshops, Chester, 1973
Newly delivered ERG 281 stands at Crosville's Central Workshop, as delivered, in NBC's leaf green bus livery; they were all repainted in the correct half green/white soon after. ERG 281 would be a long-term allocation to Wrexham Garage, surviving long enough to be part of the Crosville (Wales) fleet.

ERL 290 (NFM 290L), Swettenham nr Congleton
Only four bus-bodied Bristol REs that were new to Crosville were fitted with Leyland engines: ERL 289–290. ERL 290 works the K74 Congleton to Lower Withington, a single Saturday-only service that ran via Swettenham (Post Office), where ERL 290 is seen turning after running down to the hamlet. (Pete Thorley)

ERL 295 (BFM 295L)

Crosville's coach order for 1973 comprised Bristol RELHs with bodies fitted from Plaxton (CRL 293 – 302) and ECW (CRL 303 – 311). Downgraded to dual-purpose, ERL 295 carries a version of the NBC venetian blind livery, lettered 'Town Lynx'. Crosville modified this livery a number of times before eventual privatisation.

CRL 299 (BFM 299L), Victoria Coach Station, 1977

Displaying the National white livery in which these coaches were delivered new, Plaxton-bodied CRL 299 arrives at its destination after the long journey from the North West.

ERL 308 (SFM 308M), Wrexham Bus Station, 23 Jan. 1982

Downgraded to dual-purpose, ERL 308 was fitted with the ECW body. Some of these vehicles carried the corporate NBC half white/green DP livery before receiving company variations, which incorporated the Town Lynx cat character in varying sizes.

ELL 317 (RMA 317P), Cheltenham Coach Station

By 1976, Plaxton had introduced a restyled Panorama Elite body. The 1976/7 Leyland Leopard batch of CLL 312–327 had bodies by Plaxton (CLL 312 – 318) and Duple (CLL 319 – 327). Delivered in National white, by the early 1980s many would be downgraded to local coach status. Liverpool Garage's ELL 317 works the National Express journey to 621 into Cheltenham Coach Station, though it's got a bit further to go as Swansea is given as its destination on a piece of paper in the windscreen. CLL 317 was downgraded to dual-purpose in May 1980 and painted in local coach livery as ELL 317; it later moved to Chester and then Aberystwyth, where it carried 'DeCambria' fleet names.

ELL 314 (RMA 312P), Brecon, Apr. 1982
Downgraded to dual-purpose, ELL 314 stands in Brecon while working the lengthy 700 'TrawsCambria' service from Bangor via Dolgellau and Newtown. These services were operated jointly with National Welsh.

CLL 321 (YTU 321S), Cardiff, National Welsh Garage, 1979
New in August 1977, CLL 321 stands at one of the National Welsh garages in Cardiff, prior to the long journey back to Liverpool. Five of this batch of nine were transferred to National Travel West Fleet in March 1980, CLL 321 becoming N161.

ELL 330 (JMB 330T), Dover, 1982

The 1978 intake of coaches, again on Leyland Leopard chassis, had Duple Dominant forty-nine-seat bodies, which Duple had restyled at the front and rear. Originally CLL 330 had been downgraded to dual-purpose as ELL 330 in April 1982. It is seen a long way from its garage at Llandudno Junction, in Dover while on tour work.

CLL 333 (JMB 333T), Wrexham Garage, 1978

Brand-new CLL 333 is seen at its home, Wrexham Garage. Ten were delivered, CLL 328–337; some were re-classed as dual-purpose and repainted in NBC half white/green livery, including CLL 333 (as ELL 333) in 1981/2.

ELL 333 (JMB 333T), Blackpool Coliseum Coach Station, 1984

ELL 333 is seen again, at Blackpool, in one of at least three versions of the dual-purpose livery this vehicle would carry. Either side are coaches of JF Huxleys of Threapwood, a village close to the Welsh border near Malpas.

EMG 349 (239 FFM), Crewe Garage, 1973

Crosville was a large user of the Bristol MW, taking 236 into stock over a period of several years. The vehicles had a complex history of downgrading from coach to bus, bus-bodied dual-purpose vehicles and coach versions in three distinct body styles. Thirty-three were delivered as bus-bodied dual-purpose vehicles and were identifiable by the additional chrome bright work. EMG 349 was allocated to Crewe in the early 1970s; by the middle of the decade the type was generally only found in service at Welsh garages. EMG 349 would move to Caernarvon Garage in 1975.

EMG 355 (245 FFM), Nantwich Bus Station, 1973

EMG 355 is another of Crewe Garage's dual-purpose Bristol MWs. The K46 service ran to Wettenhall twice a day on Tuesday and Thursday only, and on Saturdays ran short, turning around at Worleston Station. EMG 355 was later allocated to Wrexham Garage.

SNG 374 (GMB 374T), Nantwich Lake, Early 1980s

The K60 was a Nantwich–Whitchurch three-days-a-week service, though not all services ran all the way through. Formerly the K53, Crewe Garage's SNG 374 works a short working to Newhall. Part of a batch of seventy-eight Leyland National B49Fs delivered from 1978–79 (SNL 340 – 417), by this time the vehicle had been re-engined with a Gardner engine, and renumbered to SNG. The company also took delivery of B series Leyland National B44Fs at the same time. (Pete Thorley)

SNL 379 (GMB 379T), Tremadog, Mid-1980s

Another vehicle that had received a Gardner engine was SNG 379. Here it stands at Tremadog, a short distance from its destination at Porthmadog. (Pete Thorley)

SNL 381 (GMB 381T), Northwich Garage Yard, 1979

In company with a number of dual-purpose Leyland Nationals and a former NWRCC Daimler Fleetline, this is Northwich Garage's SNL 381.

SNG 390 (GMB 390T), Chepstow Town Centre, 1984

Painted with the deeper white band introduced in the early 1980s, SNL 390 was newly allocated to Northwich Garage in 1978. It was converted to a Gardner engine in 1984, becoming SNG 390 at Crewe. At the unlikely location of Chepstow, it is seen on loan to National Welsh to demonstrate the new engine. After privatisation it passed to Midland Red North and after several users it survives in preservation in original NBC green livery.

SNL 391 (GMB 391T), Machynlleth Station

Aberystwyth Garage's SNL 391 stands at Machynlleth Station, ready to work the S13 to Aberystwyth. The Crosville garage was on the opposite side of the road, which in 1982 had an allocation of seven vehicles, all single-deck. (Pete Thorley)

SNG 414 (LMA 414T), near Weston Rhyn

Another re-engined Leyland National, Oswestry Garage's SNG 414 works near the English/Welsh border on the D60 Oswestry to Weston Rhyn/Bronygarth, all of which are in Shropshire. (Pete Thorley)

SMG 394 (851 RFM), Aberystwyth Garage, June 1976

Bristol MW SMG 394 was an ECW B41F bus version from new. Seen in unrelieved NBC green livery, it was allocated to Aberystwyth Garage until July 1976, when it was transferred to United Automobile, becoming their 2305 until disposal in December 1977.

SMG 409 (429 EFM), Runcorn Garage, *c.* 1975

The roof lights give a clue to the origin of SMG 409, delivered to Crosville as coach CMG 409 in July 1961. It was downgraded in 1971 to one-man-operation and re-seated to B43F, though the single-leaf coach door was retained. The company had recorded this as busway staff transport (G409) in 1976, which I suspect was when this photo was taken, though it retained its full fleet plate. In 1979, it would be cut down by the company, becoming recovery vehicle G409, for Northwich Garage.

EMG 418 (914 VFM), Flint Garage, 7 Jan. 1974

Like other NBC constituents, Crosville had some indecision over corporate liveries around their introduction in 1972. Two of the bus-bodied dual-purpose vehicles, EMG 415 and 581, were correctly painted in NBC corporate half white/green by Wrexham Garage in 1972 but were soon repainted in bus green livery. The vehicles retained the EMG fleet plate, so they were classed as dual-purpose by the company. Here is EMG 418 in unrelieved green.

EMG 427 (808 XFM), Chester Bus Station

From 1962, Crosville took delivery of Bristol MWs with a new-style coach body. 808 XFM, as CMG 427, had carried a cream and black coach livery when new. By 1972, it had been downgraded and fitted for one-man-operation. EMG 427 finished service as a staff transport, or 'shunt bus' as the company called them.

SMG 438 (1216 FM), Llangybi, 28 Mar. 1973

New at the same time as EMG 427, seen above, SMG 438 was a bus from new. Seen in surroundings that typify much of Crosville's rural Welsh operations, SMG 438 works the S6 from Aberystwyth to Lampeter, though it may have been a short working as Llangybi is displayed.

SMG 447 (1226 FM), Oswestry Station

In the same batch as SMG 438, SMG 447 is seen outside the former Oswestry Railway Station, where the company's only Shropshire garage was also located. The batch SMG 437 – 451 had B41F bodies. In the background is one of the unpopular (with drivers) ex-United Counties Bristol LHs. SLL 993 (XBD 406J) had come to Crosville in 1978.

SMG 465 (1246 FM), Anglesey, 1976

The next Bristol MWs delivered, numbered SMG 452 – 466, seated forty-five. At this time, Crosville listed vehicles used by the three garages on the island as simply Anglesey-allocated. SMG 465 works the N6 Holyhead–Amlwch cross-island service. SMG 465 would be withdrawn in 1979, passing to Silcox of Pembroke Dock, who used it until 1983.

SMG 466 (1247 FM), Shrewsbury Bus Station, 1975

In Midland Red territory, Crosville's D75 had worked into the town from Llanidloes via Newtown and Welshpool. Shrewsbury was as far north-west as Midland Red's huge operating area covered and this area of Shropshire was also served by a number of independents, on both sides of the border. SMG 466 was listed at Wrexham Garage in 1976.

EMG 473 (2178 FM), Macclesfield Bus Station, *c*. 1974

In 1972, Macclesfield Garage and services were transferred from North Western to Crosville. Its allocation was made up of types all unfamiliar to Crosville. EMG 473 was transferred to the garage soon after takeover and, though typical to Crosville, must have been out of place in these parts of Cheshire! By 1976, EMG 473 had been transferred to another taken-over location, the ex-Western Welsh Garage at Newcastle Emlyn on the opposite side of Crosville's vast operating area.

CMG 492 (2199 FM), Chester Bus Station, 1974

An illustration of the complex changes to this batch. In the early 1970s, this batch was re-painted in dual-purpose livery with the roof light painted over, initially with the large yellow pre-corporate fleetnames below the windows; then, as seen here, with corporate fleetnames in the usual position. After this downgrading, they incorrectly retained their CMG plates. Then, confusingly, in the mid-1970s the entire batch was repainted in bus green and received new EMG plates, instead of the correct SMG classification. CMG 492 stands in the parking area opposite the bus stands at Delemere St Bus Station, waiting to work the long H21 Liverpool via Runcorn service.

SMG 507 (BFM 438B), Wrexham Garage

The 1964 intake of Bristol MWs totalled twenty-five. The first thirteen, SMG 497 – 509, had bus bodies as seen here, and the final twelve, CMG 510 – 522, were fitted with the coach body as shown by the vehicle partly visible in the background. Strangely, a number of this batch were withdrawn before the much older Bristol MWs still in service.

ELL 509 (OMA 509V), Aberaeron Garage, Apr. 1982

1979 saw a second delivery of Leyland Leopards with Duple Dominant C49F bodies (CLL/ELL 497 – 511). Delivered new in both National white and corporate dual-purpose green/white, they were allocated to garages right across the company's area. ELL 509 received 'DeCambria' fleetnames for its services from Aberaeron Garage.

ELL 518 (LJX 818H), Northwich Bus Station, 1980

The early 1980s saw the company purchase a number of second-hand, coach-bodied, dual-purpose vehicles. The first batch were six Plaxton Panorama Elite C47F-bodied Leyland Leopard PSU3A/4RTS, numbered ELL 517 – 522 and were purchased from National Travel (East) in 1980, though they were new to Hebble. ELL 518 was one of two allocated to Northwich, probably finding use on the long-running Barclays Bank contract service.

ELL 520 (LJX 820H), Aust Services, 1983

ELL 520 is seen in Aust Services, beside the Severn Bridge on the M5, along with National Welsh and NT South West coaches. Aust Services had been an interchange point for National Express services for the South West and South Wales. The six were allocated to Northwich (two), Mold, Aberystwyth (ELL 520) and Pwllheli (two).

ELL 524 (UTF 727M), Victoria Coach Station, 1984

Two more second-hand DP vehicles, this time from Ribble, Leyland Leopard PSU3B/4Rs with Duple Dominant C49F bodies, were purchased in 1982. Numbered ELL 523 (XTF 801L) and ELL 524 (UTF 727M), they were allocated to Northwich for a time and used on the Barclay Bank contract services. (Richard Morant)

ERL 528 (PTF 716L), Derby Bus Station, 1983

The last batch of the dual-purpose second-hand purchases again came from Ribble, Bristol RELH6Ls with ECW C47F bodies. Looking like Crosville's own ERL types, ERL 525 – 530 (PTF 710/714 – 16/711-12L) entered service in 1983, all in NBC local coach livery. All would receive venetian blind town lynx livery except ERL 525, which was painted in the National Express version. Macclesfield Garage's ERL 528 works the 201 Derby–Manchester service; note the centred fleetnames.

CRG 531 (AFM 106B), Chester Bus Station

CRG 531 is pressed into service on the long 925 National Express Caernarfon–Glasgow service. CRG 531 was in a batch of six (CRG 524 – 532) new in 1964. (Pete Thorley)

SMG 542 (EFM 623C), Mold Garage, July 1976

1965 saw Crosville take delivery of another twenty-three Bristol MWs with ECW B45F bodywork (SMG 533 – 555). Typifying the batch, SMG 542 of Mold Garage has a plain front, but some of this batch had a small lower grill. SMG 542 would be converted to staff transport bus G542 in 1980, for use at Runcorn until final withdrawal in 1981.

CMG 565 (HFM 565D), Cheltenham Coach Station, 1974

Another batch of vehicles that was painted into dual-purpose livery briefly, but re-painted in National white soon after, was the 1966 delivery of Bristol MWs, CMG 557–570, totalling fifteen. CMG 565 is seen in Cheltenham Coach Station, connecting with the extensive Associated Motorways network.

CMG 566 (HFM 566D), Red & White Ross-on-Wye Garage, 1976

Seen after repainting into National white, CMG 566 of Wrexham Garage is standing outside the Red & White garage at Ross-on-Wye, while on tour work in the region. CMG would be sold to a dealer, Martin's (Middlewich), in 1980. I remember returning from a day trip to Blackpool in one of these coaches when the open roof light flew off on the M6; we all shuffled up and the driver carried on unperturbed!

CRG 573 (HFM 573D), Wrexham Garage, Late 1970s

Crosville, like many NBC constituents, tried to match registrations to fleet numbers and the 1966 delivery of CRG 571 – 580 did match. CRG 573 spent much of its time at Wrexham, being fitted with single-leaf coach doors; this batch never received dual-purpose livery. CRG 573 survives in preservation.

EMG 583 (HFM 583D), Sealand Road Workshops, Chester, 1975

Crosville's last delivery of bus-bodied Bristol MWs in 1966 totalled twelve (EMG/SMG 581 – 592); half the batch were dual-purpose. One of the local coach batch, EMG 583 was allocated to Aberystwyth Garage in 1976 and would be withdrawn in 1979.

EMG 584 (HFM 584D), Aberystwyth Garage, 1976

Seen at its home garage, EMG 584's coach seats are visible in this 1976 view. Similar to a number of other Crosville Bristol MWs, this vehicle found further use as a service vehicle, becoming G584, for staff transport at Runcorn, in which role it served until May 1982.

ERG 594 (HFM 594D), Chester Bus Station

Crosville bought three Bristol RELL6G/ECW DP50Fs in 1966 (ERG593 – 595) for the 'Cymru Coastliner' service. The holders for the slip boards are still in place. They are unusual in that they were built with the short-lived curved front design. The next three delivered in 1967 (ERG 596–598) featured the same body but with a flat front. ERG 593 was allocated to Heswall Garage at the time. (Pete Thorley)

ERG 596 (NFM 596E), Nantwich Bus Station

Crewe's ERG 596 loads at Nantwich Bus Station for the K64 Nantwich Circular service, which ran to Hack Green and Sound on a Thursday, Friday and Saturday, at 10.25 and 13.45 only. (Pete Thorley)

SNL 594 (JTU 594T), Pwllheli Garage

The Leyland National 'B' series was introduced as a low-cost version of the type, easily identifiable by the lack of the distinctive roof pod. Crosville took delivery of the type when it was introduced; seventy-five were delivered in 1978/9 (SNL 556–600 and SNL 641–670). SNL 594 stands inside Pwllheli Garage in 1982.

SLL 610 (LMA 610P) and SLL 602 (KMA 532N), Sealand Road Workshops, Chester, Aug. 1975

Two new Bristol LH6Ls, SLL 610 and 602, await entry into service at Crosville's Central Repair Workshops in Sealand Road. Crosville took forty of these Bristol LHs with the revised curved front (SLL 601 – 640); the first six had unmatched registrations, and from SLL 611 they received 'CA' registrations issued by Denbighshire, probably as Cheshire plates were not available. SLL 602 was allocated to Crewe and SLL 610 entered use from Northwich Garage.

SLL 622 (OCA 622P), Sealand Road Workshops, Chester, Sep. 1975

Another new Bristol LH6L, SLL 622 awaits entry into service for at Biddulph Garage. Bought as a replacement for the Bristol MW and for some of the non-standard types brought into the fleet with NBC reorganisations, they were found in many Welsh garages and at Crewe, Northwich, Biddulph and Macclesfield.

SLL 640 (OCA 640P), Wrexham Garage, July 1976

The last of the Bristol LHs to be purchased by the company, SLL 640 stands inside Wrexham Garage in 1977. Wrexham was one of Crosville's largest garages, with a huge parking area at the rear. Just visible is one of Crosville's Land Rover service vehicles.

SNL 646 (GMB 646T), Aberystwyth Garage, 1985

Crosville took two batches of the new Leyland National B in 1978, including SNL 641, the pre-production prototype. SNL 646 was in the second numbered batch of thirty (SNL 641 – 670). The B series were the first short, 10.3 m Leyland Nationals in the company's fleet. Very much a replacement for the Bristol MWs, here long-term Aberystwyth-allocated example stands outside the garage. Note the Crosville Leyland Sherpa van behind, carrying additional lettering to advertise commercial services.

SSG 649 (646 LFM), Bangor Garage, 11 June 1974

A number of Crosville SC4LKs lasted long enough to receive NBC corporate livery. The company had bus (SSG) and coach variants, the latter having coach seats and different grill mouldings (CSG), though both were finished in bus livery. One of the bus type, SSG 649 is seen ready to work the M77 Bangor to Rhilwas.

SSG 672 (246 SFM), Rhyl Garage, 1973

SSG 672 stands in Rhyl Garage yard in the unrelieved green that was applied under the directive of the NBC corporate scheme. Seventy-nine Bristol SC4LKs were delivered to Crosville between 1957 and 1961. Associated with Welsh garages, a number were temporarily allocated to Warrington Garage while the infamous Dunham Massey canal aqueduct was being rebuilt, and the diversion route only allowed the use of these lightweight buses. These vehicles were all withdrawn by 1975.

CVT 682 (NFM 682E), Llandudno, 1975

Though very much a Bristol/ECW fleet, Crosville took delivery of ten lightweight Bedford VAM coaches in 1967. CVT 681 – 686 were fitted with Duple Northern bodywork, as seen on CVT 682, still in dual-purpose livery.

CVT 682 (NFM 682E), Llandudno Junction Garage, 1976

CVT 682 is seen again at its home garage. By this time, the company was repainting all the CVT/CVF coaches in National white. Note one of the Plaxton-bodied coaches in the background. Used mainly on tour work in North Wales, which they were ideally suited for, they would all be disposed of by 1979.

CVT 687 (NFM 687E), Sealand Road Workshops, Chester, 1973

The last four of the 1967 delivery, CVT 687 – 690, were fitted with Plaxton C45F bodies. In common with some other Crosville coaches, the entire batch was painted in dual-purpose livery in 1972/3 before a reversal of fortune saw them all repainted in National white. CVT 687 awaits its return to Rhyl Garage.

CVT 689 (NFM 689E), Llandudno Junction Garage, Jan. 1977

CVT 689 awaits use outside Llandudno Junction Garage. The Bedford coaches were allocated to Ellesmere Port, Oswestry, Rhyl (six) Aberystwth and Llandudno Junction (five).

CVF 693 (XFM 693E), Llandudno Junction Garage, 1974

In 1969, the company took four more Bedford VAMs, CVF 691 – 694, fitted with Duple C45F bodywork, which was strikingly different to the batch delivered two years previously. Initially painted in local coach livery, all were repainted in National coach white soon after.

CVF 693 (XFM 693E), Northwich Garage, 1979

CVF 693 is seen again now in the National coach white, into which all the Bedfords were repainted, after a brief period in local coach livery. CVF 693 and 694 were two lightweight Bedfords that were transferred to Northwich Garage in the late 1970s for use on Barclays Bank contract service.

MTF 701 (CLG 701S)

Long before they became commonplace, Crosville had experience using minibuses, with two rail replacement Commers in the 1960s. Between 1976 and 1983, the company purchased two Ford Transits (MTF 700/1), a Bedford (MRB 702) and a Dodge (MDP 705). Some were used on the 'Unchaled Community Bus' services; the second Ford Transit, MTF 701, was used on the N60 Beaumaris service, necessitated by limited clearances on the road at a village en route. (Pete Thorley)

EPG 704 (KFM 704J), Wrexham Garage, *c.* **1985**

Crosville's choice of 102 Seddon Pennines has become infamous (EPG701–750/SPG 751–800). A unique type for an NBC constituent, purchased because the usual choice of vehicle were unavailable, they were not as successful as hoped; nevertheless they remained in use for a decade. Crosville gained two more (SPG699/700) as a compensation from Seddon. Apart from the not-quite-up-to-spec dual-purpose variants, they seemed okay! Here, EPG 704 stands withdrawn at the back of Wrexham Garage.

EPG 714 (KFM 714J), Rhyl Garage, 1981

Looking a bit worse for wear, EPG 714 stands in the yard of Rhyl Garage, carrying Wrexham local identity. Behind is a Leyland Leopard ELL316, originally a National white coach downgraded to dual-purpose in 1980.

EPG 719 (OFM 719K), PMT Newcastle Garage, 1976

Crewe out-stationed a few vehicles at the neighbouring Potteries Motor Traction (PMT) Newcastle-under-Lyme Garage for operating its K52 Madeley, K65 Whitchurch and K66 Knighton services. All three were on the extremity of the Crosville map, starting and finishing outside Crosville's operating area. At this time Crewe had an allocation of seven dual-purpose and four bus Seddons.

EPG 746 (OFM 746K), West Kirby, Greenbank Road, 26 May 1981

EPG 746 stand in the parking area used at West Kirby. One of the fifty dual-purpose versions, the seats only differed from the bus version in the material used. The other vehicles are ENL 851, SPG 778, SPG 787, SNL 809 and EPG 703.

SPG 780 (OFM 780K), Runcorn Garage

The fifty bus versions of the Seddon Pennine were delivered as a dual-door B45D variant. They were ideal for services on the Runcorn Busway, on which SPG 780 of Runcorn Garage would spend its time. Crosville rebuilt a number to single-door in the late 1970s.

SNL 806 (WFM 806L), RAF Sealand, 1972

Crosville was one of the first NBC companies to take delivery of the new Leyland National. The first batch in 1972 were twenty-four dual-door examples, SNL 801 – 824. Flint Garage's SNL 806, still with bare metal bumpers, passes RAF Sealand in 1972. The A55 service ran between Sealand and Holywell via Flint.

SNL 822 (WFM 822L), Chester Bus Station, 1976
Liverpool Garage's SNL 822 departs from Chester Bus Station for the long journey home via Runcorn. This is not the ideal vehicle for this service, which would be better suited to a dual-purpose Leyland National.

ENL 896 (GMA 399N), Chester Bus Station, 1974
Between 1972 and 1975, Crosville took delivery of 177 Leyland Nationals. Twenty-two were dual-door buses, twenty-five were single-door bus versions, and the remainder were dual-purpose like ENL 896, seen here. ENL 896 is still fitted with a Leyland badge, with the fleetplate unusually above. These badges were replaced by the small coloured double-N symbol in the mid-1970s.

ENL 904 (GMA 407N), Chester Bus Station, 1975

Crosville was the NBC's largest user of dual-purpose Leyland Nationals, eventually totalling 128 examples, all 11.3 m DP48F versions. The prestigious L1 'Cymru Coastliner' was an ideal service for these new vehicles. With a fitment to carry the yellow 'limited stop' headboard, Caernarfon-allocated ENL 906 stands on the parking area opposite Chester Bus Station.

ENL 911 (HCA 971N), Wrexham Garage, 6 Aug. 1977

In 1974 all eighteen deliveries of Leyland National were DP48F versions; the pod had been reduced in size on these vehicles. One of eight allocated to Wrexham, ENL 911, stands in the yard at the rear of the garage.

ENL 913 (HCA 973N), Chester Bus Station, 1975

The first of the sixty-six dual-purpose Leyland Nationals delivered in the 1975 order, ENL 913 of Llandudno Junction Garage, arrives at its destination after the long journey along the North Wales coast. It is displaying the L1 'Cymru Coastliner' headboard, which necessitated moving the Leyland symbol to the lower panel. Note that the Double N symbol is still green at this time.

ENL 922 (HFM 178N), Bangor, Early 1980s

Caernarfon Garage's ENL 922 works L1 'Cymru Coastliner' out of Bangor part-way into its 76-mile journey along the North Wales coast. This service had been introduced in September 1965, using newly delivered Bristol REs, forming an hourly service that passengers paid for on the bus, no bookings necessary, as Crosville stated on their literature. The through-service has been lost to privatisation; today it would require two changes.

ENL 925 (HFM 181N), Wrexham Garage, 15 June 1983

Wrexham Garage's ENL 925 stands in the large yard area at the rear of the garage. A long-term resident of this garage, it had been used for local work when seen in June 1983.

ENL 959 (MLG 959P), Bangor, Feb. 1984

With its green front, Rhyl Garage's ENL 959 could be mistaken for one of the bus batch of Leyland Nationals. Actually a dual-purpose version, which carried all-over advertising for S4C, the Welsh-language Channel 4, it had the 'Cymru Coastliner' lettering incorporated into the livery, which would only be appropriate when operating the service, as seen here at Bangor.

SNL 983 (YTU 983S), Winsford Town Centre

In 1977, Crosville took delivery of eight more Leyland Nationals, originally planned to be B series types; instead, 11.3 m A series were delivered, numbered SNL 979–986. SNL 983 of Northwich Garage loads in Winsford. (Pete Thorley)

SNL 993 (LMO 223L), Rhyl Railway Station, 1984

The registration gives this Leyland National away as not being new to Crosville. SNL 993–998 were purchased from Alder Valley in 1984. SNL 993 had been Alder Valley 101, new in 1973, and works the M44 from Rhyl to Abergele.

STL 901 (KDB 695), Macclesfield Bus Station, 4 Aug. 1972

Initially all numbered in the 900 series, Crosville purchased vehicles from other NBC companies in 1972, some through regional boundary changes, others to help with vehicle shortages. Former North Western batch STL 901 – 916 were Leyland Tiger Cubs, fitted with MCW B44F (STL 901 – 905) or Willowbrook (STL 906 – 916) bodies. STL 901 was in a batch of five, two of which were soon withdrawn, possibly before receiving a coat of green paint. In use with Crosville, STL 901 is seen before it received fleet plates; it would be withdrawn in 1974.

STL 901 (KDB 695), Macclesfield Garage, 1974

STL 901 is seen again, but in leaf green and with corporate fleet names.

STL 905 (KDB 700), Macclesfield Railway Station, 1974

Ex-North Western STL 905 also received corporate fleetnames, and a cream, as opposed to white, central band. Note the rear wheel still in NWRCC red.

STL 911 (LDB 769), Northwich Garage, 1973

Stood with other ex-North Western vehicles, STL 911 shows the Willowbrook-style body fitted to STL 906 – 916. Upon painting into green, the majority of this type received the short-lived large yellow Crosville fleet names below the windows. STL 911 was withdrawn in 1974.

STL 914 (LDB 773), Northwich Bus Station, 2 June 1973
New in 1958, LDB 773 was 773 in the North Western fleet, a Leyland PSUC1/2 with a Willowbrook DP41F body. Crosville classed these as buses when they were taken over in January 1972. A couple of the ex-NWRCC vehicles survived as static offices at the company's garages at Runcorn and Liverpool.

CLL 918 (VDB 962), Northwich Garage Yard, 1973
Of the thirteen Leyland Leopards CLL 917 – 926, two were fitted with Plaxton C49F bodywork (CLL 918 – 919) and the remainder were finished with the stylish Alexander Y type body. Looking very smart recently repainted in NBC local coach livery, but not yet renumbered, CLL 918 stands outside its home garage.

ELL 325 (FJA 219B), Blackpool Coliseum Coach Station, 1977

ELL 325 (formerly CLL 925) carries Alexander bodywork painted into local coach livery. These vehicles retained their CLL classification until renumbered ELL 317/320 – 329 in 1975, to avoid duplication with newly delivered Leyland Nationals. Four of this type were cut down at Sealand Road to become recovery vehicles.

CLL 927 (FJA 221B), Blackpool Central Coach Park, 1974

CLL 927 (later ELL 327) is seen parked at Blackpool after working the X26 from Harriseahead, a location just outside Biddulph in Staffordshire. Operated jointly with Potteries Motor Traction (PMT), it ran via Biddulph, Congleton and Lytham in the summer months only. This vehicle was not rebuilt into a towing vehicle.

STL 930 (MUH 146), Aberystwyth Garage, 1972

Eleven Leyland Tiger Cubs were purchased from Western Welsh in 1972 and they had five body types: Weymann B44F (STL 930); Park Royal B43F (STL 931 – 932, 935 – 939); Park Royal B41F (STL 934); Metro Cammell B41F (STL 933) and Marshall B41F (STL 940). STL 930, still in WWOC livery but with Crosville fleet plates applied, stands in Aberystwyth Garage yard soon after transfer. This bus became towing vehicle L930 at this garage in March 1974, though it was probably already used in this role, and was later painted in unrelieved leaf green. It was sold to the dealer Martins (Middlewich) in November 1976.

STL 933 (UKG 274), Sealand Road Workshops, Chester, 1973

The sole Metro Cammell example, STL 933 is seen after a visit to Sealand Road, awaiting its return to Newcastle Emlyn Garage. It did receive a white waistband before being withdrawn in April 1976. After further use in Eire, it survives and is currently being restored for preservation. The two ex-South Wales Transport AEC Reliance/Willowbrook B41F buses, SAA 983/4, were similar to this type.

STL 934 (DBO 344C), Aberystwyth Garage

STL 934 stands at Aberystwyth Garage, the sole ex-WWOC example with a Park Royal DP41F body, though it was classed as a bus by Crosville. It is painted leaf green and is complete with corporate fleetnames.

STL 939 (FUH 363C), Carmarthen, 1975

Ex-Western Welsh STL 939, which was in the batch fitted with Park Royal B43F bodywork (STL 931–932, 935 – 939), departs from Carmarthen on the S44 service to Cardigan. This service was Crosville's most south-westerly route. Vehicles were allocated to the former WWOC garage at Newcastle Emlyn, itself the most remote company location from Chester at a distance of 130 miles. (Richard Morant)

SLL 941 (HHD 866), Northwich, 1974

Crosville purchased five Leyland Leopard/Marshall B53Fs from Yorkshire Woollen District in 1972. Numbered SLL 941–945, they were allocated to Northwich Garage, probably to help with vehicle shortages around the time of the transfer of North Western operation in Cheshire in 1972. Crosville probably chose these vehicles as they were similar to the North Western vehicles operated by Northwich Garage, so staff were familiar with their operation. All received the large yellow fleetnames on the side, but only SLL 941 received corporate fleet names. (Richard Morant)

SAA 985 (LDB 746), Macclesfield Bus Station, Aug. 1972

Crosville received fifteen AEC Reliances from North Western in 1972. They were in four body types: Willowbrook B43F (SAA 985 – 988), Alexander B41F (SAA 989 – 990), Willowbrook B53F (SAA 991 – 995) and Willowbrook DP51F (EAA 996 – 999). SAA 985 was similar in appearance to the Leyland Tiger Cub STL 906 – 916 batch.

EPG 745 (OFM 745K), Runcorn Garage, 1975

Dual-purpose Seddon Pennine EPG 745, along with three Bristol RE buses, stands in the maintenance area of the then new Runcorn Garage. Beechwood Garage was opened in November 1975 to serve the dedicated 'Busway' system. It had replaced Runcorn's earlier Broadway Garage.

ENL 919 (HFM 175N), Bangor Garage, 30 July 1985

Dual-purpose Leyland National ENL 919 and Bova Futura CBD 62 (B62 DMB) stand outside the garage at Beech Road, Bangor. Opened in 1931 as one of the company's larger facilities, it was similar in appearance to Liverpool Edge Lane Garage.

EAA 999, Macclesfield Bus Station, 1974

Ex-North Western Willowbrook-bodied AEC Reliances SAA 991–995 and EAA 996–999 had similar bodywork, external differences being that the dual-purpose vehicles had a broad chrome trim. The dual-purpose vehicles, though classed as such by Crosville, were all painted plain green, with large yellow fleetnames. Of the dual-purpose batch, only EAA 999, seen here, received NBC corporate fleet names.

DFG 27 (308 PFM), Liverpool Pier Head, 1974

Crosville had a large fleet of Bristol Lodekkas; DFG 27 was a FS6G Gardner-engined version. Allocated to Liverpool Garage, the vehicles allocated within the Merseyside PTE area carried their symbol after the fleet name, as seen here. The H3 was a Warrington – Rainhill service. Crosville had a large garage in Liverpool and extensive services to the Wirral and eastwards towards Runcorn and Warrington. (Transport Library)

DFG 72 (882 VFM), Rhyl, Early 1980s

Crosville took delivery of Bristol Lodekkas in long and short front-loader and rear-entrance versions, all in the same years of 1961–63. Thirty of the FSF version were new in 1961/2, and later three would be converted (DFG 68/72/81) to open-top for the 'sea front service', serving holiday resorts along the North Wales coast. Working the M81 service from Rhyl to Pines Caravan Park, which ran every thirty minutes in the summer months, DFG 72 carries the white livery used for these vehicles introduced in the late 1970s. The 'sea front' services covered the stretch between Deganwy and Prestatyn. (Pete Thorley)

DFG 90 (900 VFM), Liverpool Pier Head, 1979

The H3 service again, this time with a Bristol FLF6G, DFG 90, which appears to have lost its fleet plates! The FLF had seventy seats, as opposed to sixty in a Bristol FS.

DOG 105 (GFM 105X), Frankby, near West Kirby, Mid-1980s

Crosville took 175 Leyland Olympians between 1982 and 1984. They were a common sight on inter-urban service between Chester and Birkenhead, and around Merseyside. With the red sandstone of the Wirral prominent, DOG 105 works a joint MPTE service 80A from Birkenhead to West Kirby. (Pete Thorley)

DOG 119 (MTU 119Y), Llyn Peninsula, Mid-1980s

Though allocated to Welsh garages as well, DOG 119 looks somewhat out of place as it works the Pwllheli to Abersoch service, across the remote Llyn Peninsula. (Pete Thorley)

DOG 119 (MTU 119Y), Rhyl Railway Station, *c.* 1982

DOG 101–130 had their chassis built at Bristol; the remainder were Workington-built chassis. All were bodied by ECW at Lowestoft. DOG 119 works the L1 limited stop Chester–Caernarfon, the 'Cymru Coastliner'. Crosville would purchase twelve similar vehicles in 1985, but as dual-purpose vehicles, EOG 201 – 12. These would be some of the last vehicles purchased by the nationalised company. (Pete Thorley)

DFG 122 (1202 FM), Wrexham Bus Station

DFG 122 pulls into Wrexham Bus Station alongside DFG 236 and DFB 228. DFG 122 was new in 1963 from a 1962/3 batch of nineteen with Gardner and Bristol engines (DFG/DFB 119 – 148).

DFG 150 (AFM 113B), Caernarfon, 3 Oct. 1973

An unusual variant of the Bristol Lodekka FLF6B, DFG 150 was completed as a CH55FD coach. Still painted in Crosville pre-corporate livery, three of these were purchased in 1964 and used on North Wales limited stop services that became the 'Cymru Coastliner'. Note that the additional trim incorporates the fleetname, and the luggage rack visible in the rear window.

DFG 163 (BFM 433B), Liverpool Pier Head, 1977

1964/5 saw a large intake of Bristol FS6B/G with ECW H60RD bodies. Liverpool DFG 163 has just worked from Warrington on the H1 service, which ran in arrangement with MPTE as a limited stop within its area.

DFG 165 (BFM 435B), Liverpool Pier Head
DFG 165 stands among other Crosville vehicles, including a Leyland National and a low-roof Bristol RE. This location was also called Mann Island and was Crosville's main terminus in the city.

DFG 175 (DFM 211C), Chester Bus Station, 1977
With the Northgate Arena being built in the background, DFG 175 stands on the parking area across from the bays at Chester Bus Station, ready to work the A3 service to Rhyl, which will take the best part of two hours.

DFG 195 (GFM 195C), Wrexham Bus Station, 1982

The rear-entrance Bristol Lodekka was a common sight along the North Wales coast, Chester, Merseyside and Wrexham. Wrexham was one of the last locations to see them in regular service. Wrexham Garage's DFG 195 stands in the bus station, with ex-Southdown Daimler Fleetline/Northern Counties HDG 900; both carry the Wrexham local area fleetnames.

DFG 197 (GFM 197C), Chester Bus Station, 1977

In the same location as DFG 175 above, Wrexham Garage's DFG 197 starts its one hour, thirty-six minutes service to Llangollen. Requiring crew operation, these vehicles worked the Chester–Wrexham services into the late 1970s. (Transport Library)

DFB 202 (GFM 202C)

Crosville took only five Bristol Lodekka FLFs in 1965 (DFB 199–203). DFB 202 is seen on an enthusiast excursion and carries an inaccurate destination blind. In 1976, DFB 202 and two others were allocated to West Kirby Garage. (Pete Thorley)

DFG 235 (JFM 235D), Barmouth

The 1966 Bristol Lodekka FS intake was DFB/G 204 – 238. Here, DFG 235 of Wrexham and Bristol FLF DFB 250 of Bangor stand in the well-known location alongside the railway line at Barmouth. Both wait while working excursion traffic to Harlech Market. DFG 235 was a Bristol Lodekka FS6G. (Pete Thorley)

DFG 245 (SFM 245F), Liverpool City Centre

The last delivery of Bristol FLF6B/GS was the 1966/7 batch of twenty-five (DFB 239 – DFG 263). Crosville's DFG 245 is closely followed by MPTE Leyland Atlantean L507 (507 KD), as it works the joint service 76 to Prescot. Liverpool, having its own PTE bus company, had a joint agreement with the NBC subsidiaries Ribble and Crosville. This involved a limited stop service with the MPTE boundaries.

DVG 271 (HTU 160N), Liverpool Pier Head, 1976

Between the 1967 batch of Bristol FLFs (DFG 239 – 263) and 1975, Crosville took no new double-deck vehicles into stock. The company was a late taker of the Bristol VRT and DVG 271, seen above, was in the first batch of 1975 (DVG 264 – 286). These early Bristol VRTs were still fitted with the pressed metal fleet plate, before grey transfers became standard. Note this Mk 2 version had protruding moulding lines around the lights.

DVG 276 (MDM 276P), Sealand Road Works, 1975

DVG 276 is seen brand new at SRW in 1975, still to be fitted with fleet plates. DVG 276 was Crosville's first Mk 3 version, identifiable by the lack of protruding moulding lines around the lights. Crosville did not take delivery of the flat-fronted Mk 1 version from new, though later had a number of second-hand early VRTs.

DVL 288 (RLG 288P), Rock Ferry Garage, Mar. 1977

The second batch of Bristol VRTs was the first 1976 delivery of six (DVL 287 – 292), but fitted with a Leyland engine. 1976 would also see another batch of twenty Bristol VRTs (DVL 321 – 340). This was the last batch to be fitted with metal fleet plates.

DDG 303 (FJA 190D), Northwich Bus Station, 1974

Nineteen Daimler Fleetlines with Alexander bodies came with the North Western services in 1972 (DDG 301 – 319). They could be found at all three of the former NWRCC depots. By the 1980s, they started to be allocated to other garages, including Crewe, Wrexham, Mold, Flint and Chester, though only one – or in the case of Chester, two vehicles.

DDG 307 (FJA 194D), Northwich Garage, 1973

Still in NWRCC red, DDG 307 leaves Northwich Garage with repainted STL 914, an SRL, Bristol RE and a DAA, AEC Renown, all ex-NWRCC vehicles. The remains of the former company name can be seen on the garage front.

DDG 307 (FJA 194D), Northwich Garage, 1975

DDG 307 is seen again but now repainted in full NBC corporate livery. Northwich Garage and bus station were located together, with a large open parking area at the end of the site. Northwich Garage also had a paint shop, which was accessed from a road at the rear.

DDG 319 (JDB 254F), Biddulph Garage, Oct. 1976

Standing between a PMT bus and a Crosville Marshall-bodied Bristol RE, ex-NWRCC DDG 319 was the last of the batch of Daimler Fleetlines transferred in 1972. Biddulph was a former NWRCC garage, shared with PMT. This arrangement continued after 1972, though it would then be a mix of red and green vehicles.

DVL 395 (JMB 395T), Liverpool Garage

Though the company did not take delivery of its first Bristol VRT until 1975, eventually by 1981, it would take 242 new vehicles into stock. DVL 395 stands outside Liverpool Garage after working from Rainhill.

DVL 398 (JMB 398T), Macclesfield Garage, 1982

DVL 398 is seen parked with DVL 414/413, all locally allocated. These were part of a large batch of seventy-five Bristol VRTs (DVG/DVL 341 – 425) fitted with Gardner or Leyland engines that were delivered between 1977 and 1979.

DEG 402 (RDB 897), Warrington Arpley Bus Station, 1976

Another non-standard type that came from North Western were the eleven Dennis Loline IIIs fitted with Alexander H71FD bodies (DEG 401-411). All eleven of this type were allocated to Macclesfield Garage when taken over from NWRCC, though seven DEGs had moved to Warrington Garage for their final year of operation. DEG 402 stands at the Arpley Bus Station.

DEG 404 (RDB 899), Northwich Bus Station, 4 Aug. 1972

DEG 404 was an early withdrawal of the eleven Dennis Lolines. Only lasting until 1974, here it is seen with the short-lived large yellow fleet name, which many ex-NWRCC buses received before the NBC corporate livery was introduced.

DAA 501 (VDB 964), Northwich Garage Yard, 1973

The third type of double-decker transferred from NWRCC were the sixteen AEC Renown/Park Royal H74FDs, DAA 501–16. Like DAA 501, the majority were allocated to Northwich Garage, with Biddulph and Macclesfield having one each (May 1976). Thought out-of-use when seen here, DAA 501 survived until early 1979, when the type disappeared from Crosville use.

DVG 558 (SMS 37H), Amwlch Garage, 1983

From 1981, Crosville took a number of early flat-fronted Bristol VRTs from several operators including United, Southdown, Ribble, East Midland and Eastern National, though these were new to the Scottish Bus Group. One of the latter, DVG 558, was new to Alexander (Midland) in 1971 and is seen outside Amwlch Garage. No doubt these students would be surprised to see themselves featured thirty-six years later!

DLG 874 (831 AFM)

Even in the mid-1970s, Crosville had a large number of Bristol Lodekka LD6B/GS, numbered DLB/G 787 – 982. They had been introduced between 1955 and 1959, the majority had been withdrawn by 1976. DLG 874 works D2 and is seen en route between Oswestry and Wrexham/Chester in the mid-1970s.

DLG 871 (828 AFM), Colwyn Bay, 1977

DLG 871 was converted by the company into open-top in 1977. Displaying the white livery that was adopted for Crosville's open-top fleet, rear-entrance Bristol Lodekka DLG 871 is seen on the M17, one service that operated in this form in the summer months. It was sold to Martins (Middlewich) in June 1979.

HDG 903 (TCD 373J), Chester City Centre

The purchase of fourteen Daimler Fleetlines with Northern Counties bodies (HDG 900–914) second-hand from Southdown in 1980 necessitated the introduction of a new prefix letter for the body type. All Crosville double-deck vehicles had previously been low-height; these vehicles were high-bridge, so the letter H was used to ensure the additional height was noted. Departing on a local service, HDG 903 carries the company's anniversary logo in front of the double-N symbol. It is followed by Chester Corporation buses. Six would later be converted to open-top for use on North Wales open-top seafront services.

HDL 919 (XUF 389K), Caernarfon Garage, May 1984

Also in 1980, Crosville purchased another batch of fifteen Daimler Fleetlines but with ECW H74F bodywork (HDL 915 – 929). These also came from Southdown.

HVG 934 (OWE 274K), Sealand Road Works, June 1983

Completing the 1980 second-hand purchase were six Bristol VRTs with East Lancs H73F bodies (HVG 931–936, originally DVG 11–16). New to South Yorkshire PTE in 1972, these were a distinctly non-NBC type; they could be found at garages including Liverpool, Rock Ferry and Aberystwyth.

45A (CFM 724L), Chester Bus Station, Mid-1970s

A very rare view of Austin Marina 7 cwt van 45A. Allocated to the head office at Crane Wharf (Chester), it had replaced a Ford Escort van, 44A, in April 1973. 45A was disposed of in 1979. The company would own two other similar vans, 95A and 96A. At least one was disposed of by Martins (Middlewich), where I saw it with accident damage *c.* 1980. (Pete Thorley)

50A (TFM 632K) and 49A (KRN 193H), Sealand Road Works, Mid-1970s

Two Bedford KEL lorries at Sealand Road in the mid-1970s. 50A was a stores lorry new in April 1972, replacing a similar Bedford with the same body. The company owned two pantechnicon lorries, usually finished with hand-painted advertising on the side panels; they were used to transport vehicle spares. In the background is 49A, another Bedford, new in 1970 to Ribble; it was transferred to Crosville in August 1975, lasting only until April 1977. (Pete Thorley)

51A (NMB 441V), Sealand Road Works, Mid-1970s

From the mid-1960s, Crosville had used the Bedford K series for its lorries, both open and pantechnicon, changing to the replacement Bedford TL in the 1980s. 51A was fitted with an Atlas hydraulic crane and is seen here at the central workshops, a location always guaranteed to produce a good selection of service vehicles. (Merfyn Jones)

68A (A448 UMA), Sealand Road Works, 8 Dec. 1984

68A was a Bedford TL fitted with a small HIAB crane, one of three delivered in 1984. Only a few months old, it is seen at Sealand Road Central Workshops. The majority of the large lorries were allocated to Sealand Road, with one allocated to Wrexham Garage. 68A was disposed of to Martin (Middlewich). (Merfyn Jones)

59A (002 FM), Sealand Road Works, 1979

Crosville's heavy recovery vehicle was an ex-military AEC Matador, impressively rebuilt by the company in 1957. Numbered 59A, it operated on trade plates 002FM/259FM from the central workshop in Sealand Road, Chester. Around 1986, it was moved to Llandudno Junction Garage in preparation for the split to Crosville (Wales). It finished its time abandoned at Aberystwyth Garage; luckily it was saved for preservation – amazingly this vehicle is seventy-five years old in 2020! Crosville purchased a second Matador in July 1984 from Eastern National (0101), numbering it 60A, so Crosville (England) could maintain this capability.

66A (TFM 389M), Macclesfield Garage, 1980

The company had thirteen Land Rovers (including three from NWRCC). 66A, which had been allocated to Runcorn Garage, was moved to Macclesfield to replace an ex-NWRCC Land Rover, 78A (SDB 764J), in 1980. (Merfyn Jones)

89A (XCA 173R), Rock Ferry Garage, 1977

Like all NBC constituents, Crosville maintained a fleet of commercial vehicles for service use. In the 1960s it had favoured Fords for its vans, both Escorts and Transits, but in the early 1970s it started to purchase Bedford or Austin (Leyland) vehicles. Leyland Sherpa 89A served at Rock Ferry Garage.

91A (OMA 304Y), Chester Bus Station, Mid-1980s

Rock Ferry Garage's 91A was a Mk 2 Leyland Sherpa. Note the 'engineering department' lettering on the door, common to most of Crosville's Sherpa vans. This van also carried registration 611 LFM (from DLG 1) and later PMA 760Y. The company chose the Sherpa for its medium size right up to the 1986 privatisation and for some time after. (Pete Thorley)

83A (DEY 823X), Sealand Road Works, Chester

Morris 440/575 van 83A was unusual with its Bangor registration, allocated to SRW and later Macclesfield. After a period with no small vans, the company purchased several British Leyland (Morris) and Metro vans. (Merfyn Jones)

G410 (ACA 125A), Bangor Garage, 1984

Formerly bus SMG 410, G410 carried its original registration, 430 UFM, until 1984 when it gained ACA 125A, perhaps to retain a cherished registration. The company would convert a total of ten Bristol MWs to towing vehicles, two with bus bodies and eight with the former coach body, as seen on G410 at Bangor Garage.

G815 (XFM 227), Chester Garage, 1975

Bristol LD6G G815 was an early conversion to driver training vehicle with the lettering contained in the standard size white stripe between the decks. It is seen inside Chester Garage. Converted in October 1975, it was withdrawn in May 1982.

G816 (XFM 228), Chester Bus Station

Another Bristol LD, G816 illustrates the broad white band that became the standard trainer livery. Used from Wrexham Garage, it had been converted in October 1975 and lasted until October 1983.

MO17 (JFM 991), Sealand Road, Dec. 1973

MO17 was one of two mobile offices converted from 1949 chassisless Beadle buses. It was out of use when seen at Sealand Road in 1973. The other, JFM 990, is preserved in working condition.

L317 (VDB 961), Warrington Garage, 1976

Crosville converted four ex-NWRCC Leyland Leopards to towing vehicles in 1976. L317, seen here, was used briefly at Mold/Flint before allocation to Warrington Garage; others were L320 at Crewe, L321 at Runcorn and L322 at Liverpool.

L320 (AJA 142B), Crewe Garage, 1978

Leyland Leopard towing vehicle conversion L320 is seen outside Crewe Garage in 1978. Interestingly, the four conversions all went to garages that were always Crosville, while the ex-NWRCC garages at Northwich and Macclesfield received Bristol MW towing vehicles G409 and G360 respectively.